Breakfast Bites

2-MINUTE DEVOTIONS TO START YOUR DAY

BroadStreet PUBLISHING

BroadStreet Publishing Group LLC
Racine, Wisconsin, USA
Broadstreetpublishing.com

Breakfast Bites

© 2018 by BroadStreet Publishing

ISBN 978-1-4245-5582-6 (hardcover)
ISBN 978-1-4245-5673-1 (ebook)

Design by Chris Garborg | garborgdesign.com
Edited and compiled by Michelle Winger | literallyprecise.com

Printed in China.

18 19 20 21 22 23   7 6 5 4 3 2 1

Introduction

Start each morning the best possible way!
Your heart will be filled with the fruit of the Spirit
and your eyes focused on God as you spend two
minutes pondering his love for you.

Enjoy devotions that are meaningful and practical,
helping you discover how to serve God with all
you have and encourage others throughout the day.
Embrace God's love, peace, and joy each morning
and let it change your outlook for the day.

MAKE MY DAY

Fill us with your love every morning.
Then we will sing and rejoice all our lives.

PSALM 90:14 NCV

Seek him first. Why is this such a recurring suggestion, both in the Bible and among Christians? If you regularly begin your day with the Lord, you already know what a day-maker he is. If you haven't settled into the practice, start today. See how his loving presence affects your days.

Before the day has a chance to disappoint you, before the enemy finds a way to distract you, seek God first. Invite him into every waking moment. Sense him in your interactions and your transactions. Notice the tenderness with which he sees the people you encounter. Invite him to contribute to your decisions. Observe how he consistently places you on the path of love. Allow him to carry your burdens and see if a joyful song doesn't swell inside you. Allow it to overtake your heart.

Jesus, I invite you to make my day today. Let my words, my thoughts, and my actions be yours. Replace my irritations and frustrations with your patience and compassion. Fill me with your love, so I may reflect it to others. Fill my heart with your song.

New studies are showing that up to 58 percent of the general population skips breakfast at least once a week! Breakfast helps give you the energy you need to make it through the day. And if you are feeling particularly crabby, it's more important than ever to eat in the morning. A good breakfast helps you face the day with more energy, and it helps you cope with some of those irksome issues that are bound to arise.

JUST PRAY

Then he prays to God, and is accepted by him,
he comes into his presence with joy,
and God repays him for his righteousness.

Job 33:26 NRSV

It's easy to become overwhelmed by expectations. We want to fit in and to belong, but the formula is constantly changing, and it's hard to know whose standards we should shoot for: family, work, friends, society, social media…who decides what's acceptable?

Look carefully at the verse this morning. What must we do in order to be accepted by God? Are we required to have our acts together, our sinful habits conquered, our church attendance perfect? No. Just pray. We pray to God, and he welcomes us in. Scrubbed and shiny, or worse for wear, it's all the same to him. He sees you, he hears you, and he invites you into his joyful presence.

Father, help me to remember yours is the standard of acceptance that matters most, and that just by praying I've already met it. Thank you for loving me as I am. Help me to remember this as I go about my day.

Many people enjoy the quiet
in the morning, and studies show
that solitary reflection
can improve concentration.

ASK ANYTHING

This is the confidence we have in approaching God: that if we ask anything according to his will, he hears us. And if we know that he hears us—whatever we ask—we know that we have what we asked of him.

1 John 5:14-15 NIV

Think of a time you wanted something, maybe from a parent or your boss, but you were too afraid to ask. Why were you afraid? Perhaps you feared you didn't deserve it. Or possibly, you wanted it, but you also knew it wasn't necessarily good for you. Whether you're an adult asking for a day off of work or a teenager asking for permission to stretch a curfew, it can be difficult to ask boldly for what you want — especially if you're not entirely certain you should have it.

Take heart in these words from 1 John and know that when you place your relationship with God as your top priority, you can ask him for anything. Anything! When we most desire to be in his will, he gladly grants our other requests.

God, you are my deepest desire. Knowing I can come to you with my needs, my dreams, and my unspoken longings brings comfort to my soul. Boldly this morning, I lay my requests at your feet. I know the answer will be just what I need.

Manakish is a popular breakfast served in Israel, Syria, Palestine, Lebanon, and Jordan. It's a flatbread topped with za'atar, which is a blend of Middle Eastern herbs and sesame seeds. Manakish is also often covered with cheese, tomatoes, spinach, or minced lamb.

YOUR WAYS

Keep me from looking at worthless things.
Let me live by your word.

PSALM 119:37 NCV

Think of a food you enjoyed as a child that you no longer find palatable, or a childhood game so simple that you can scarcely believe how many hours you once whiled away, enthralled. Where before we couldn't even taste extra sugar, our faces now contort from the overwhelming sweetness. Tic-Tac-Toe is only fun if you go first, and even then it's only fun for a round or two. With maturity comes discernment.

Examine your current life through God's eyes. Are there things clamoring for your attention that, when held up to the lens of eternity with the Father, lose their luster? Might some of the discontentment you feel in your daily life be eliminated simply by losing your taste for things that don't really matter?

Lord, I pray these words over my life: Turn my eyes from looking at worthless things! I want to follow your gaze and see what you see. I know yours is the way of life, and it is life—real life—that I crave this morning.

Some kids don't like to eat very much in the mornings, but their growing bodies need quality food to fuel their day. In fact, studies show that children who eat a nutritious breakfast benefit from improved concentration, problem-solving skills, and hand-eye coordination.

YOU ARE GIFTED

If the whole body were an eye, where would the hearing be? If the whole body were hearing, where would the sense of smell be? But as it is, God arranged the members in the body, each one of them, as he chose.

1 Corinthians 12:17-18 NRSV

Has a captivating singer, speaker, or dancer ever brought up a longing in you to perform at their level? Or perhaps a brilliant piece of art stirred up a desire to create something beautiful with your own hands? Such temporary feelings are natural; beauty is inspiring! But if we hold onto a desire to possess someone else's gifts, we run the risk of forgetting about—or never discovering—our own.

Spend some time thinking about what makes you special. If this makes you uncomfortable, or if you aren't sure, recall a time you felt particularly alive, or a time when things just seemed to be clicking. What were you doing? Begin there and ask God to show you how to do your special task for his glory.

Father, everything from your hands is good and special, and that includes me. Help me to remember this, especially on the days it feels like everyone has more to offer than I do. Light a fire in me to explore, develop, and use my uniqueness to glorify you today.

The early bird gets the worm, indeed.
Research shows that early risers are proactive,
organized, good at anticipating and correcting problems,
and tend to be optimistic.

CLAIM YOUR PEACE

I know how to live when I am poor, and I know how to live when I have plenty. I have learned the secret of being happy at any time in everything that happens, when I have enough to eat and when I go hungry, when I have more than I need and when I do not have enough. I can do all things through Christ, because he gives me strength.

PHILIPPIANS 4:12-13 NCV

Can you imagine experiencing the same level of happiness and contentment upon learning your job is being eliminated as you would upon getting an unexpected raise or promotion? The implication of these verses is simply extraordinary.

The wonderful news is that we can all experience what this verse encourages. The contentedness that comes from knowing Christ is in unlimited supply; there's more than enough to go around. In fact, the more of us who claim it, the more his strength, peace, and happiness increase. Whether it's a morning of plenty or a morning of want, claim your peace today and share the hope it gives you.

Jesus, I've learned the secret to happiness, and I want in! I invite you to take over my emotions and to send contentment into every part of my life, so that no matter what circumstances I may face, I face them with your strength, and I experience nothing but your joy.

A simple, morning stretching session does the body good. It improves circulation to the muscles and the brain, improves flexibility, sharpens concentration, and encourages better posture.

SEEK TO DO GOOD

See that none of you repays evil for evil,
but always seek to do good to one another and to all.

1 THESSALONIANS 5:15 NRSV

For a small child, a shove from another gets a shove in
return, a cruel word for a cruel word. They can't help it;
self-defense is an innate reaction to an attack. What these
little ones don't know yet but learn quickly is that regardless
of who strikes first, both are punished. In our weaker
moments, this natural impulse can rear its destructive head
in our adult lives as well. "She said what? Oh, really? Well let
me tell you about her issues…"

When we allow ugliness into our hearts, it takes up
residence, and it invites its friends—bitterness, loneliness,
and rage—to move in as well. They spread out, taking up
more and more space, crowding out the peace, patience, and
goodness of Jesus. This is why we must "seek to do good to
one another and to all," not because we'll be punished, but so
our hearts will be filled with the vitalizing gifts of the Spirit.

Holy Spirit, fill me with your fruit this morning! I need the love, joy, peace, patience, kindness, goodness, faithfulness, gentleness, and self-control you bring, so that no matter what is done to me, I can respond as I should.

Research indicates that those who make their bed every morning benefit from increased productivity, a sense of well-being, and steady adherence to a budget.

YES, PLEASE!

With this in mind, we constantly pray for you, that our God may make you worthy of his calling, and that by his power he may bring to fruition your every desire for goodness and your every deed prompted by faith.

2 Thessalonians 1:11 NIV

There is so much to feel encouraged about in this wonderful prayer from Paul to the Thessalonians! Do you have a group of women to pray and study the Word with? If you don't, pray that God would lead you to one, and then keep your eyes and heart open. If you already have a study group, you know how beautiful it is to receive prayers from someone and to pray for someone in return. Taking our focus off of ourselves blesses us in unique and surprising ways.

Even more encouraging is the content of Paul's prayer: We are worthy of God's calling, we desire goodness, and we are prompted by faith in everything we do, so that faith succeeds. Can you say, "Yes, please" to that this morning?

Oh, God, yes, please! I want to be worthy of your calling, to be equipped to do all that I can to bring you glory. I pray that everything I do to express, share, and increase my love for you would succeed. For others who are reading this today, I pray the same. Make us a force of light and goodness in the world. Bless our actions and increase our faith this morning.

If you begin a task before others are awake, you are less likely to be distracted. Start your day with a project that requires your full focus, and you're much more likely to complete it than if you started that same task midday.

CONSIDER HIS HAND

Behold, I am doing a new thing;
now it springs forth, do you not perceive it?
I will make a way in the wilderness
and rivers in the desert.

ISAIAH 43:19 ESV

When hiking through a state or national park on a well-worn, carefully laid out trail, we don't usually consider all the work that went into creating that path. If you wander off the path for just a minute or two, you start to gain an appreciation for the vast amount of effort spent and the countless hours required to remove the branches, brambles, and roots along the way. Flipping on a faucet, we don't often give much thought to the source of the water, or the many places in the world where a single faucet would be nothing short of a miracle to an entire community.

God's work in our lives, though just as intricate, can go similarly unnoticed. Take some time this morning to consider every obstacle he's removed for you to have the life you have. Marvel at how he can pull a spring up out of nothing and sustain you just because he wants to. Just because he loves you.

God, you are incredible. When I stop to consider my life, the millions of obstacles you've removed, and the continual sustenance you've provided me, it blows my mind. How deeply I am loved, how carefully you consider me! Thank you for all you have done and will continue to do for me.

If you've ever owned a cat, you've probably been woken up by its loud meowing early in the morning, or maybe it was pawing your face and kneading your chest. While this may be irritating, cats can't help it; it's in their DNA. Their ancestral wildcats wake early in the morning to hunt for breakfast because that's when their prey is most active.

AS YOU WILL

I rise before dawn and cry for help;
I hope in your words.

PSALM 119:147 ESV

For an early-morning person, these words are relatable, and perhaps even unremarkable. For those who favor the snooze button, rising before dawn seems highly overrated. How do those who love their sleep get past the opening phrase and lay claim to the power and promise in this verse?

They meet the day. They open their eyes, and their thoughts go straight to the Lord. Before anyone or anything has an opportunity to crowd their thoughts with obligation, worry, or entertainment, they bring themselves authentically before God. They go to his Word and let him speak to them there. They find their hope before anything else finds them.

Help me, Father God. I run to meet you this morning. Help me love, listen, and learn well today. Before anything or anyone else can say a word, let me hear from you. This is where my hope lies, in these first minutes, when we are all there is. See me as I am, and make me as you will.

Bananas are the most popular breakfast fruit in the United States; in fact, they're so popular that the average American eats twenty-eight pounds of bananas per year! Bananas are low in calories and contain no fat, sodium, or cholesterol. They're also an excellent source of vitamins C and B6, potassium, and fiber.

HATE EVIL

You who love the LORD, hate evil!
He protects the lives of his godly people
and rescues them from the power of the wicked.

PSALM 97:10 NLT

You turn on the news in the morning, or open a newspaper, and every day it's full of the same stories. Atrocities around the world are committed each day. By now, it's become so normal that we are sometimes immune to it. Until it affects our lives directly, we might not even notice it.

We are asked to hate evil. We aren't told to merely put up with evil, or to make sure that we don't let it bother us. We are supposed to loathe it. What does that mean for us? It means that we should pray for those who are affected by such evil, and we should look for ways to help. God will deliver them from the hand of the wicked, but he needs his armies here on earth to do their part. Together, let's offer hope to those who are suffering.

Lord, thank you for guarding me from evil. I pray for those who are troubled today, and I pray that they may see your light. Show me how I can pray specifically this morning. Help me to be aware of the needs of others today instead of just my own.

The earliest known newspaper was commissioned by Julius Caesar who had announcements carved into metal or stone and displayed in public. Today, printed newspapers are becoming a thing of the past as digital news becomes more popular. The most recent data shows that as of 2014, only 1,331 daily newspapers remained in print.

ABUNDANT RAIN

Be glad, O children of Zion,
*and rejoice in the L**ORD** your God,*
for he has given the early rain for your vindication;
he has poured down for you abundant rain,
the early and the latter rain, as before.

JOEL 2:23 ESV

Our God is so good and so faithful. He provides us with everything we need if we look to him for it. When our lives are in drought, parched from our daily grind, he sends us rain in abundance to nourish our souls and keep us from drying out. The fields that are our lives begin to green again after a season of turning brown. We feel refreshed as his showers of love pour down and over us.

Let's celebrate and be glad this morning! Our God in heaven cares for us so much. He wants to see our trees bearing fruit, and he will continue to give us what we need to nourish and grow. Turn to him when you are feeling parched, and he will give you rain.

Lord, thank you for protecting me from drying out. You give me everything I need to flourish, and for that I give you all the praise. Refresh me this morning, so I may continue to bear good fruit for your glory.

Showering in the morning has its advantages. Not only do morning showers give you an opportunity to organize your thoughts before the day begins, but they also have an energizing effect—especially if you're willing to make the water cold.

WILDEST DREAMS

To him who is able to do far more abundantly than all that we ask or think, according to the power at work within us, to him be glory in the church and in Christ Jesus throughout all generations, forever and ever.

Ephesians 3:20-21 ESV

Picture the most amazing things you could imagine actually coming to fruition in your life. Imagine your wildest dreams realized and your greatest hopes come true. Guess what? It's all possible through God. He can accomplish more than you could ever think to ask for. Do you know what else is true? He wants to do it through you.

God has given us the gift of the Holy Spirit living within us, guiding us, pressing us on toward achieving great things. He deserves all the glory and all the credit for the good we see around us. Let's praise him together and give him the honor. He is so good to us!

Father, you really are good. Thank you for using me to attain greatness for your kingdom. I know that I'm able to accomplish so much more with you than I ever could on my own. Give me big dreams this morning and the faith to believe that you will help me accomplish them.

Most people forget fifty percent of their dreams within the first five minutes of waking up, and ninety percent forget within ten minutes. If you want to remember more of your dreams, sleep experts suggest keeping a dream journal near your bed and writing in it as soon as you wake up.

WORKING WITH JOY

Whatever you do, do your work heartily, as for the Lord rather than for men, knowing that from the Lord you will receive the reward of the inheritance. It is the Lord Christ whom you serve.

Colossians 3:23-24 NASB

We are each called to do different work, whether it's working behind a desk, caring for children, cleaning a home, or selling products. Sometimes the daily work routine can be exhausting. You may not want to do it wholeheartedly. Perhaps you just want to get through the day and be done. When you serve a heavenly master, there's a reward greater than a paycheck. You are promised an inheritance that's better than anything you can imagine.

Put your mind to working with joy this morning. Work with a thankful, servant's heart knowing that your effort is seen and appreciated, and that you are serving one who loves you beyond comparison. You'll be surprised at how this shift in mindset can change your life—starting today!

Lord, I want to serve you. I'm excited to receive my inheritance from you. Help me work with my whole heart while I wait for my reward. Give me grace to walk through this day of work with joy.

Need an extra jolt from your coffee this morning? Choose a light or blonde roast. The longer a coffee bean is roasted, the less caffeine it contains, so dark roast coffee actually contains less caffeine than light roast coffee.

A BEAUTIFUL SOUND

To choose life is to love the LORD your God, obey him,
and stay close to him. He is your life, and he will let
you live many years in the land, the land he promised
to give your ancestors Abraham, Isaac, and Jacob.

DEUTERONOMY 30:20 NCV

We were created to enjoy the sound of beautiful things. We listen to music, we smile at the sound of children's laughter, and we enjoy the sweet melody of birds chirping on a crisp spring morning. But the most beautiful sound of all is the sound of God's voice speaking to us. We can hear him if we listen.

God is life. He is the source of everything. Sing with him this morning—a new song of gratitude and love. Listen for his voice. He is calling you with sounds of pure beauty.

Father, thank you for your voice. Help me choose to obey you when you speak to me, and help me hold fast to your teachings. Let me hear your beautiful whispers of love and life throughout the day.

What makes a sunrise so beautiful? A phenomenon called scattering. Particles and molecules in the air cause light rays to scatter. Short wavelengths, like blue and purple, are more affected by these particles than longer wavelengths, like red and orange. When the sun is low on the horizon, the light rays have to travel through more particles closer to the ground, and these particles scatter the blue and purple light rays, leaving us with the beautiful red and orange colors we associate with sunrises and sunsets.

FEAST OF LOVE

O taste and see that the LORD is good;
How blessed is the man who takes refuge in Him!

PSALM 34:8 NASB

Let's be honest, there are few things better than a delicious breakfast. Close your eyes and picture your favorite morning foods all laid out on a table before you. What dishes do you see? Blueberry pancakes? Bagels with cream cheese? Cinnamon French toast? A spinach and cheese omelet? Whatever your dishes may be, they are nothing compared to the feast of love that is found in a relationship with God. It tastes better than anything you've ever known.

The best part about this feast is that you can indulge in it whenever you want, any time—day or night. It's calorie free, and it's good for you. So go ahead; taste and see that the Lord is good. He's the best, and he wants to share all that he has with you.

God, I want to taste all that you desire for me. Let me share in your feast of heavenly goodness. Let me desire you above all else and take refuge in your love. Thank you for your blessings, both small and large—including my breakfast this morning!

The United Kingdom serves a traditional breakfast named the "Full English." This meal includes poached or fried eggs, sausages, bacon, fried bread or toast, tomatoes, mushrooms, and baked beans. With all that food, it's no surprise that an average Full English contains almost an entire day's calories (approximately 1,190).

NOTHING WRONG

Since we have been made right in God's sight by faith in his promises, we can have real peace with him because of what Jesus Christ our Lord has done for us.

<small>ROMANS 5:1 TLB</small>

What does complete peace look like? Perhaps it would mean waking from a good night's sleep without having anxious thoughts of the day ahead. Maybe it would mean financial stability or domestic harmony. Job insecurity, family reconciliation, or depression might plague us, but peace brings the relief we've been praying for.

When we believe that God's promises for us are true, we can trust in the peace we gain through Jesus. When he is Lord of our hearts, we are no longer separated from God because of sin. We are brought into his family and counted as sons and daughters. One of the greatest benefits in God's family is the great peace that rests with us. Nothing is wrong if we are right with God. Everything else will pass away, but his promise remains: We belong to him, and he never lets us go.

God, set my feet firmly on the peaceful promise I have through your Son, Jesus Christ. This morning, let my worries and fears be handed over to you, so that peace will take their place.

In 1960, the average American slept eight hours a night. Today, an American is more likely to sleep for only six and a half hours. Over the last one hundred years, Americans have suffered a 20 percent decrease in their nightly amount of sleep.

A PERFECT PATH

All Scripture is inspired by God and is useful to teach us what is true and to make us realize what is wrong in our lives. It corrects us when we are wrong and teaches us to do what is right. God uses it to prepare and equip his people to do every good work.

2 Timothy 3:16-17 NLT

God freely shares the secret to finding our life's great purpose and our reason for existence. For millennia, people have searched for it, and some search without ever finding a satisfactory answer. God isn't trying to confuse us or delay the fulfillment of our purpose on earth. He wants us to understand it and pursue it with passion.

The Word of God contains every answer we will ever need. It is a divine tool meant to show us our path. In it, we find correction and rebuke but also encouragement and great wisdom. If we are humble enough to receive it, God's Word will equip us for our greatest purpose: serving one another for the kingdom of heaven.

Heavenly Father, you have a great plan for my life. Thank you for your perfect path. I ask for the humility to submit to your Word, to obey your voice, and to walk with endurance to fulfill my purpose. Help me to start by reading your Word this morning before I begin my busy day.

We all know the countless benefits of exercise, but those who work out in the morning gain extra perks. Exercise before noon can help kick start weight loss and boost your mood for the day. If you have a hard time getting out of bed, you're more likely to hit the gym if you have an exercise partner and lay out your clothes the night before.

MORNING PAUSE

Enter his gates with thanksgiving
and his courts with praise;
give thanks to him and praise his name.

PSALM 100:4 NIV

The morning wake-up call came too soon today. Whether it was in the form of children, an alarm clock, or a heavy, restless heart, your slumber is over. Your mind immediately starts going over your to-do list for the day as you stumble through your morning routine. You glance at your watch. How can you already be running late?

It is at this moment that you must stop to thank God. That's right, actually stop what you are doing, get down on your knees, and thank him. A thankful heart prepares the way for you to connect rightly with God's heart. He isn't someone we use to get what we want. He is a sincere, loving provider for everything you will ever need. Pausing to thank him gives him the honor he's due. But it also kisses your heart with peace and joy in the midst of busy morning routines.

Loving Father, I enter into your presence now on another one of your creations—this day. Thank you for giving me another morning on earth. Thank you for life in my body. Help me walk in an attitude of thanksgiving unto you. I love you.

To avoid sleeping through your alarm in the morning, move it across the room. That way, you're forced to get out of bed to turn it off. You can also help your body set its own internal alarm clock by waking up at the same time every day.

INWARD RENEWAL

Therefore we do not lose heart. Though outwardly we are wasting away, yet inwardly we are being renewed day by day.

2 Corinthians 4:16 NIV

Sometimes when you wake up, you don't feel rested at all. Your back might ache, there could be bags under your eyes, and your skin may seem a little (or a lot) looser. You know you don't look or feel like you did when you were younger, but you can't quite remember exactly when you started aging.

Today, own your aging instead of wishing it away. Everyone is growing older; it's nothing to be ashamed of. In many cultures, people aspire to be older because it means that they are wiser and more widely respected. More importantly, getting older in God also means that you are renewed day by day. Your goal when you wake should not be how you can alter your appearance to make yourself look younger; rather, it should be how you renew your heart, mind, and soul.

God, help me see that inward renewal is far more valuable—and eternal—than outward renewal. I give you my concern over my appearance this morning. Thank you for every moment you have given me on this earth. I choose to be thankful and joyful today.

Neuroscientists recommend that we shut our phones down at least one hour before bedtime for restorative sleep. Why? The light emitted from the screens of our devices, like smart phones and tablets, contains more blue light than natural light. Blue light is known for disrupting our brain's production of melatonin—the hormone that makes us feel sleepy.

HIDING HIS WORD

I have stored up your word in my heart,
that I might not sin against you.

PSALM 119:11 ESV

There is tremendous value in taking time to study the Word of God. It's one thing to breeze through it in the morning, but it's entirely different to chew on and to digest its teaching. When you really digest God's Word, it goes from your head into your heart.

One of the best ways to store his Word in your heart is to memorize portions of Scripture. When you memorize something, you repeat it in your head. This simple act naturally causes you to think about the Word of God more than other idle or anxious thoughts. Furthermore, the nature of *storing* means you are obtaining something now that you will need at a later date. It means you see the importance of keeping it, so that it may benefit you in the future. Start storing God's Word in your heart this morning!

Father, please give me the wisdom and grace to store your Word in my heart right now, so that it will be there in my hour of need. Help me take time to ponder your wonderful promises each morning.

It is common knowledge that the sun rises in the east, but it is perhaps less known as to why this is so. The answer is simple: As the Earth spins on its axis, it spins toward the east.

PROMISE OF FREEDOM

Jesus said to the Jews who had believed him, "If you abide in my word, you are truly my disciples, and you will know the truth, and the truth will set you free."

John 8:31-32 ESV

Some of us are incredibly blessed to live in a free country where we can express our ideas and beliefs, worship openly, and live our lives as we see fit. Constitutions have been written to ensure freedom for all citizens—national, individual, and political. There is one freedom, however, that no constitution, regardless of how comprehensive, can promise, and that is spiritual freedom. Liberation of the soul only comes through forgiveness offered to us through Christ. When our sins are forgiven, and we stay faithful to the truth, then we are truly free.

Maybe it's time for a "freedom check" this morning. Is your life truly a reflection of the Christ in whom you say you believe? Are you faithfully reading the Word and obeying it? If not, perhaps it's time to get back on track. Then you can be confident that no matter what you may face, the God of truth will guide you to freedom.

God, I want to be faithful to your Word. Forgive me when I neglect it. This morning I want to fill my mind with truth that will set me free.

When you hear "croissant," France likely comes to mind. However, the croissant originates from Austria. A popular bit of folklore from the 16th century claims that Viennese bakers heard Turkish soldiers digging a tunnel into Istanbul in the middle of the night in an attempt to siege the city. The bakers then alerted the citizens, and the legend credits the bakers for Austria's victory over the Turkish army. To celebrate, the bakers shaped their dough into a crescent, which is an emblem of the Turkish flag.

MUCH BETTER

Let me hear of your unfailing love each morning,
for I am trusting you.
Show me where to walk,
for I give myself to you.

PSALM 143:8 NLT

We all see God through the lens of humans because we are finite. When we hear of his attributes, we often put a human spin on them—many times subconsciously. If we hear that he is love, we think that means he loves like we do. If we hear that he is patient, we think of the most patient person we know. And if we hear that he is kind, we picture someone who exhibits kindness well. But in all of our human examples lies failure because at some point, even the most loving, patient, and kind person we know will fail.

We silently accuse God in our disbelief. We question the one who has never lied. We suggest he's incapable of the perfect love that he has professed. A sick feeling stirs in our gut. *At some point, this perfect love, patience, and kindness will run out.* Take hold of the truth this morning: God is much better than you think. His attributes are unmarred and untainted. He cannot fail. Let those thoughts guide you today.

Father God, thank you for being who you say you are.
This morning, help me to believe that you indeed have
the power to love without failing. I trust you to show
me where to walk today. I give myself to you
without holding back.

Granula, the first cold breakfast cereal, was invented
in 1863. It was made from Graham flour that was
twice baked and broken into nugget-like pieces, similar
to the consistency of today's Grape Nuts® cereal.
Granula was so tough that it had to soak overnight
to be soft enough to chew.

A WILLING HEART

Restore to me the joy of your salvation,
and make me willing to obey you.

PSALM 51:12 NLT

Picture a defiant little girl crying in a timeout chair. All she
has to do to be welcomed back is to admit that she drew
on the wall, or apologize for hitting her brother, or simply
eat the carrots on her plate. But she doesn't. She won't. She
can't. Unwilling to accept the entirely reasonable condition
of her parents, she wallows in her sadness. We're adults now,
but sometimes we find ourselves in that same corner. Bound
by our own rebellious choices, we pull our knees up to our
chests and wallow.

Yes, we heard God's direction, but we didn't feel like
following. We don't *like* carrots. Bob *deserved* it. It is our
choice, always, to stay in the chair, and it's our choice, always,
to get up and rejoin the party. God restores us, forgives us,
and he can even make us willing—if we can admit that we
need his help.

God, I confess it. That little girl is me. Rebellious and defiant, I ignore your will and exercise my own. Though exhilarating in the moment, my rebellion robs me of my joy. Restore me this morning to the joy of your salvation. Your way is best, and your will is perfect. Please help me remain there always.

Despite the numerous health benefits that come from eating a nutritious breakfast, such as weight control, lower cholesterol, and improved performance, 29 percent of women skip breakfast to spend more time on other aspects of their morning routines.

HELP ME GET DRESSED

God has chosen you and made you his holy people. He loves you. So you should always clothe yourselves with mercy, kindness, humility, gentleness, and patience.

COLOSSIANS 3:12 NCV

The classic nightmare we've all had at one time or another involves us forgetting to properly dress ourselves before going out in public. Everyone sees our state of immodesty and laughs. Hopefully, we wake up before the dream goes on much longer.

Starting any day without putting on the characteristics in this Scripture may well produce the same result of embarrassment. Compassion, kindness, humility, gentleness, and patience don't put themselves on us. We consciously put them on with the help of the Holy Spirit. Pride, arrogance, impatience, and judgment will rise up in our lives if we're not properly dressed. The results will damage our relationships and put us in a place we wish we could wake up from. Get dressed this morning so that you are ready to conquer the day!

Father God, today I ask that by the power of your Spirit you would clothe me with a compassionate heart and with kindness, humility, gentleness, and patience. Be glorified through me today.

Have you ever wondered what the difference is between white eggs and brown eggs? Aside from their color, there isn't one. The color of the egg depends on the breed of the hen, but there is no difference in quality, flavor, or nutritional value.

CONSIDER THE SPARROWS

"Look at the birds of the air; they neither sow nor reap nor gather into barns, and yet your heavenly Father feeds them. Are you not of more value than they? And can any of you by worrying add a single hour to your span of life?"

MATTHEW 6:26-27 NRSV

Jesus told those he taught to consider the sparrows when faced with worries of this life. He created the sparrows and the entire earth that sustains the life of the sparrows. When he used these birds as an example, he didn't simply create the comparison for his sermon preparation. Jesus created the sparrows thousands of years before he ever taught. With every ounce of intent at the point of creation, he foresaw the day that he would illustrate how to live through the sparrows.

Sparrows were designed to make beautiful sounds, to bring joy to those who watched and listened to them, and to show children of God how to live. Sparrows wake up knowing that worms will come to the surface. They fetch what they need for the day, carelessly soar around, then find some more worms and grubs when they're hungry. They go to sleep with total trust that tomorrow will be no less delightful than today.

God, thank you for the sparrows that show me how to live. Help me trust you not only this morning and throughout today, but also tomorrow morning and the morning after that. You take care of all your precious creatures, and I am one of them.

Animals that are most active at dawn and dusk are considered "crepuscular." Lots of mammals fall into this category, including bears, moose, deer, and housecats. Barn owls and nighthawks are examples of crepuscular birds, and some snakes and lizards—particularly those in desert environments—are also crepuscular creatures.

OUR CREATOR

When I look at the night sky and see the work of your fingers—
the moon and the stars you set in place—
what are mere mortals that you should think about them,
human beings that you should care for them?
Yet you made them only a little lower than God
and crowned them with glory and honor.

PSALM 8:3-5 NLT

Skydiving looks absolutely thrilling and completely terrifying. Those who have had the courage to leap from a plane say that it is an exhilarating experience that cannot be replicated. A woman shared that as she floated through the air, praise welled up in her soul as she saw God's magnificent creation from an entirely new perspective. The psalmist was just as enthralled with the mighty works of God. God created man in is his very own image with a coronation of sorts, as he crowned him with glory and honor and gave him dominion over the earth.

Are you feeling somewhat insignificant this morning and maybe a bit forgotten? Consider this: You are fearfully and wonderfully made! Your value cannot be measured. Through the vast splendor of the universe, God sees you, he thinks about you, and he cares for you. Revel in that for a moment.

Oh, God, it is amazing that you, the God of the universe, care about me! You have fashioned me in your image for a divine purpose. Help me to live in the wonder of this truth today.

Don't be afraid to enjoy the sun. Moderate sun exposure can be good for your body. Sun exposure jumpstarts vitamin D production, boosts your mood, and may protect against a range of conditions from cancer to multiple sclerosis.

PRAISE THE LORD!

Let all that I am praise the LORD.
I will praise the LORD as long as I live.
I will sing praises to my God with my dying breath.

PSALM 146:1-2 NLT

God commands us numerous times in his Word to praise him. How can he expect us to fulfill such a directive? On some days, digging through the rubble to find a nugget of gratitude seems flat out formidable. Negative thoughts can float throughout the mind like a shadowy cloud, and if allowed to remain, such thoughts can darken the entire day.

The psalmist understood. Even though his life was in constant danger, he knew that as he centered on the greatness of God, his problems were divinely solved. He wasn't engrossed in himself. He looked at God and saw him for who he was: helper, creator, promise keeper, provider, deliverer, healer, protector, and defender. Make David's words your prayer to the Lord this morning. As you do, your heart will nod "yes," and hope will arise.

Lord, you are great and worthy to be praised!
I lift my voice in praise and in thanksgiving this morning.
Be near to me today and be glorified in my life as I tell
of your goodness and love.

If you've ever heard a rooster crow, chances are that
it woke you up early in the morning. As irritating as
their song may be, roosters crow for many reasons.
Like humans, roosters have an internal clock that helps
them anticipate sunrise and begin their hunt for food.
Their crow serves as a territorial declaration
to other roosters.

TUG-OF-WAR

If you direct your heart rightly,
you will stretch out your hands toward him.
If iniquity is in your hand, put it far away,
and do not let wickedness reside in your tents.
Surely then you will lift up your face without blemish;
you will be secure, and will not fear.

JOB 11:13-15 NRSV

If you hang around kids at all, you will soon observe a fair amount of selfish behavior. They pay no attention to a certain toy until another child starts playing with it, and then it becomes a tug-of-war. In their immaturity, they focus on their own happiness without regard for anyone else's. Wouldn't you agree that when we don't get what we want, we sometimes act like children?

Are you in the middle of a tug-of-war with God this morning? Are you bucking and bristling at the circumstances he has allowed? The best decision you could make as you start your day is to surrender—lay down your own desires and demands, and let God have his way. He loves you too much to permit your way because he knows his way is better for you. There is nothing better than the peace of surrender.

Lord, this morning I surrender myself anew to you.
Forgive me for my willfulness. I put aside my selfish
agenda that contends with your plan for me.
Thank you for loving me so much!

In the book of Exodus, God instructs Moses to
accomplish many of his tasks early in the morning.
These include Moses' trek up Mount Sinai to receive
the Ten Commandments and his confrontations with the
Pharaoh. Visit the following verses: Exodus 7:15,
8:20, 9:13, and 34:2-4.

RANSOMED

I will shout for joy and sing your praises,
for you have ransomed me.

PSALM 71:23 NLT

A boy whittled a little boat out of a scrap of wood. Proud of himself for his accomplishment, he decided to test it in a stream that wound through his family's property. He ran on the bank alongside the boat, watching it bob through the water. Soon the current picked up, and away his boat went... faster than he could follow. Weeks later, as he and his dad were in town, they spied his little boat in the window of a store with a price tag on it! With joy he ran into the shop expecting to retrieve his lost boat. But alas, he would have to pay for it. In the end, the boy earned enough money to buy back what was already his.

Isn't that what Christ did for us? He made us, lost us, and then bought us back, paying for us with his life. The psalmist couldn't contain his joy as he contemplated that wonder! God has ransomed us. On this fine morning, remember to thank God for redeeming you. Shout for joy and sing his praises!

Oh, Lord, you created me, but I was lost in sin until you found me. Thank you for buying me back! Help me to sing for joy and to praise you with all that I am today.

A doughnut shop in Portland, Oregon known for its off-the-wall flavors once served doughnuts that used Nyquil and Pepto Bismol as ingredients until the U.S. Food and Drug Administration forced the shop to remove them from the menu.

THE DO-OVER

The faithful love of the LORD never ends!
His mercies never cease.
Great is his faithfulness;
his mercies begin afresh each morning.

LAMENTATIONS 3:22-23 NLT

Have you ever looked back over segments of your life and wished you could have a do-over? As time has gone by, you have gained a new perspective on the past. It is easy to see the folly of a decision and grieve over wrongdoing. The vivid memories of your past sins and failures are tough to erase, and even though you know God has forgiven you, you have not forgiven yourself. This is the spot where Satan wants you to camp.

Let's consider God's view of your predicament. First, he sees you as forgiven and chooses not to remember your sins. In addition to forgetting your past failures, his love and mercy never stop. They begin fresh every morning. Jump in the shower of God's love and mercy this morning, and remember, every time you need it, you get to have a do-over!

Jesus, I receive your faithful love and mercy this morning.
Yesterday is gone forever, and I will live today bathed
in your mercies.

People interested in losing weight may want to
prioritize their breakfast. A recent study showed that
individuals who made breakfast their largest meal of
the day lost an average of 17.8 pounds over
a three month period.

TWO ARE BETTER

Two people are better off than one, for they can help each other succeed. If one person falls, the other can reach out and help. But someone who falls alone is in real trouble. Likewise, two people lying close together can keep each other warm. But how can one be warm alone?

ECCLESIASTES 4:9-11 NLT

Sharing our struggles with others is never easy. No one likes to admit to feeling weak, lost, or broken. Instead of turning to those who could help us when we are struggling, we foolishly attempt to cover up what we are wrestling with. This only leads to isolation and a deeper place of pain. Depending on others for help is not a sign of weakness. God gave us each other for support, encouragement, understanding, and unity.

We all have our times of need, and it is critical that we share our vulnerabilities with others. It is in our vulnerability that we can see the beauty of friendship. True friends don't leave you alone in your struggles; they join your battles, fight alongside you, and pick you up when you feel too weak to take another step. They exemplify God's love for you. If you find yourself this morning in a place of weakness, seek out a friend. Refuse to hide in your struggles.

Jesus, thank you for friends with whom I can be real, honest, and open. Thank you for those who help carry me through hard times in life. Be my strength today as I walk forward in your grace and in your mercy.

People eat bacon and eggs together 71 percent of the time. Bacon is high in choline, an essential nutrient that helps fetal brain and spinal cord development. However, because bacon is high in fat, cholesterol, and sodium, smarter swaps include eggs, peanuts, and spinach.

THE GREATEST
COMMANDMENT

*"'Love the Lord your God with all your heart
and with all your soul and with all your mind.'
This is the first and greatest commandment."*

MATTHEW 22:37 NIV

If you were raised in church, you may remember being told that Jesus loved you, and you must love him, too. It sounded so simple, and you loved God in a beautifully childish way. Now, as an adult, the words may still roll off the tongue easily, but how is it really done? Obedience necessarily involves every part of our being: mind, will, and emotion. Our love for God should be reflected in our thoughts, speech, relationships, behavior, attire, and selected entertainment.

Loving God with this level of intensity cannot be done on our own. The power to live it out comes from God himself. He loved us first! Ask God for a new understanding of his love for you this morning and determine that you will love him back with everything that is in you.

Jesus, thank you for loving me with a love that cannot be measured. I want to love you back with my whole being. Help me to show my love for you in everything that I do today.

According to sleep experts, people who rise early and go to bed early benefit from more restorative sleep because their internal circadian rhythms are more in sync with the earth's clock.

GOD'S PROMISES

Don't be afraid, for I am with you.
Don't be discouraged, for I am your God.
I will strengthen you and help you.
I will hold you up with my victorious right hand.

ISAIAH 41:10 NLT

God's Word is full of wonderful promises that are often conditional: a command and a promise. Think of the parent who says to their child, "Eat all your vegetables, and I will give you some ice cream." The child is motivated to obey by the tantalizing promise. Isaiah speaks to us as God's children, and he challenges us to embrace God's offer of help and strength by meeting his conditions. He will give us strength, help, and stability if we refuse fear and discouragement. As we embrace the truth that God is ever present, powerful, and loving, we are then in a position to receive the promises he offers.

How is your outlook for this new day? Are you discouraged and fearful about the issues you are facing? Perhaps you need to remind yourself of who God is. Strong. Helpful. Powerful. Present.

God, I love your promises, and I want to experience every
one of them. Help me to uphold my part of the bargain.
I'm sorry for my disbelief, fear, and discouragement. I
choose to place my complete confidence in you
this morning.

Doughnuts have been a source of comfort to soldiers
during times of war. In World War I, "Doughnut Girls"
were women who volunteered to serve these tasty
treats to soldiers. Similarly, in World War II
and the Vietnam War, some of the women who
volunteered with the Red Cross were called
"Doughnut Dollies."

TRANSFERRED AND TRANSFORMED

He has rescued us from the kingdom of darkness and transferred us into the Kingdom of his dear Son, who purchased our freedom and forgave our sins.

COLOSSIANS 1:13-14 NLT

If you've ever traveled to a foreign country, you have probably experienced culture shock to some degree. Feelings of confusion and anxiety are common as you encounter a way of life completely different from your own. You've been transferred from one society to another. Colossians speaks of a different sort of relocation—not a physical one but a spiritual one. Through Christ's forgiveness we have been rescued from a life ruled by Satan's power and transferred to a completely new realm—to the kingdom under the headship of a loving Savior. This transference is much greater than a mere change of location; it is a transformation of our character.

We aren't where we once were, and we aren't who we once were. Take a few minutes this morning to praise God for rescuing you from darkness and for giving you a brand new life in a brand new land!

God, my heart is full of thanksgiving this morning
for the miracle of transformation. Thank you for rescuing
me from my sin and shame and for giving me eternal life.

Common breakfasts in South India include idli, sambar,
and dosa. Idli is a savory cake made from a batter of
fermented black lentils and rice. It's often served with
sambar, a vegetable and lentil-based stew.
Also served with sambar is dosa, a crepe-like food
that often contains a spicy potato filling.

A BROKEN HEART

*The LORD is near to the brokenhearted
and saves the crushed in spirit.*

PSALM 34:18 ESV

Goodbyes are possibly one of the most difficult experiences that we face—whether that's through death or a major move. Loving deeply is costly. The price Jesus paid for love was death. He understands the pain of separation—his own Father forsook him when he took on the sins of the world. But now he is at the right hand of the Father as both our intercessor and our high priest who understands our weaknesses. He knows what it's like to have a broken heart, and he rescues us.

In the course of ordinary life, there are times when we experience heartbreak for any number of reasons. It is comforting to know that Jesus understands because he, too, has been there. Be reminded this morning that he is especially close to you and will rescue your bruised spirit. Cry out to him; his ear is inclined your way!

Father, I am so grateful that you identify with my pain. Thank you for your nearness. Help me to keep trusting you until relief comes. I ask for your peace to be mine as I walk through this day.

The dread of Monday mornings is so universal that there's a term for it: the "Monday Blues." The average person doesn't crack a smile until after eleven o'clock in the morning on a Monday, and over 50 percent of employees are late to work.

FAITH WITHOUT SIGHT

It was by faith that Abraham obeyed when God called him to leave home and go to another land that God would give him as his inheritance. He went without knowing where he was going.

Hebrews 11:8 NLT

Abraham, the father of the faithful, was a man of obedience. Had he heard God's call, but disregarded it out of fear or disbelief, God could not have established a new nation through his descendants. Abraham took the risk because he was convinced that God was true, and he set out for a place he did not know. Genuine faith always obeys God. In fact, our obedience to God is the indication that our faith is real. Abraham took one step at a time before the next step was revealed.

This morning you may be following the Lord as though you are in the dark. You just don't see where he is leading you. Remember that he sees the entire picture and is engineering the circumstances of your life very carefully. He knows what he is doing, and he asks that you take just one step of faith at a time.

Oh, God, I come to you this morning to reaffirm my faith
in you. You are good and faithful, and you love me too
much to leave me directionless. Help me trust you more
and lead me in the way everlasting.

People sleep an average of ninety minutes fewer
than they did before the invention of the lightbulb.
According to lighting experts, there's an ideal lightbulb
for our bedrooms. The next time you're shopping, look
for a bulb that has 2,000–4,000 lumens and a soft
white/warm white temperature.

BLIND TRUST

You love him even though you have never seen him;
though not seeing him, you trust him; and even now
you are happy with the inexpressible joy that comes
from heaven itself. And your further reward for
trusting him will be the salvation of your souls.

I PETER 1:8-9 TLB

Is it possible to love and trust a person you have never seen?
Peter seemed to think so. Writing to Christians during
a time of great persecution under the tyrant Nero, Peter
reminded them of their faith and love for a God they had
never laid eyes on. Peter and the other apostles had the
privilege of experiencing Jesus firsthand, but these folks's
trust transcended the natural, and with eyes of faith they
experienced the inexpressible joy of their salvation.

How are you doing in the "blind trust" department? Does
God seem distant and indifferent on this fine morning?
Remember that although you cannot see God with your
physical eyes, he is very much with you. His eyes are on you,
and his ears are open to your cries. Trust him today. The
reward for trusting him will be the salvation of your soul.

Jesus, it would be so wonderful to sit down for a cup of tea with you in person, so that we could chat about all the things I'm concerned about right now. But I know you are real even though I cannot see you with my physical eyes. Thank you for being with me.

Consider drinking green tea in the morning instead of coffee. Not only does it have caffeine, but it is also loaded with antioxidants. A hot cup of green tea in the morning has been shown to improve brain function, boost metabolism, and lower your risk of cancer, cardiovascular disease, and type 2 diabetes.

CONTENTED STRENGTH

Not that I am speaking of being in need, for I have learned in whatever situation I am to be content. I know how to be brought low, and I know how to abound. In any and every circumstance, I have learned the secret of facing plenty and hunger, abundance and need. I can do all things through him who strengthens me.

PHILIPPIANS 4:11-13 NLT

Paul was a man who knew how to survive and thrive in just about any situation. He had been whipped, lashed, beaten, stoned, shipwrecked, lost, imprisoned, hungry, thirsty, and cold. Yet, in spite of it all, he had learned the secret of living contentedly by fully trusting in Christ who gave him strength.

Our problems are small in comparison but still significant to us and to God. Remember, your God would never ask something of you that he would not supply the necessary strength to accomplish. This morning, whatever is ahead of you, you can rest knowing that Christ's strength is enough to see you through—not just barely squeak by, and with contentment!

Thank you, God, for sharing Paul's secret with me. Help me to be content with my present and to fully rely on the strength you promise to provide. I can do everything because I have you.

Dog owners tend to be healthier than non-pet owners and owners of other types of pets. Dog owners participate in more aerobic exercise from walking their four-legged friends, so they typically have lower heart rates and blood pressure. Studies also show that the presence of a dog helps to reduce stress.

Stroll with your pup (or a friend's) in the morning to enjoy some health benefits and a lovely sunrise.

HE IS ENOUGH

He said to me, "My grace is sufficient for you, for my power is made perfect in weakness." Therefore I will boast all the more gladly about my weaknesses, so that Christ's power may rest on me.

2 CORINTHIANS 12:9 NIV

The doctor, a wise and devout Christian, listened compassionately as his patient's story unfolded. The woman's husband was gravely ill, and she was struggling emotionally and physically as she faced each day without much hope for the future. Then he said something that both alarmed and encouraged her: "You know, if your husband should die, you will be okay. You have Jesus."

Are you remembering that you have Jesus this morning? Today may have dawned bright and sunny, but inside all is not well in your world. Maybe the next twenty-four hours look unrelentingly gloomy. Pull yourself up. If you know Christ, you know that his grace is sufficient, his strength is made perfect in your weakness, and his presence sustains you. You are standing on solid ground that is immovable and unchanging. Christ has a grip on you—cling to him and know that he is enough!

Father, help me today. My faith is wavering, and I am unmotivated to persevere. I know your grace is sufficient for me, and your power can work in my weakness. I trust you in this moment. You are enough.

Eggs are a popular breakfast option for a reason: they're easy to prepare in an endless number of ways, and many people consider them tasty. You may not have known that eggs are also high in protein and contain all nine essential amino acids. Their nutritional efficiency makes eggs a no-brainer when it comes to a healthy breakfast.

HOPE IN GOD

So, Lord, where do I put my hope?
My only hope is in you.

PSALM 39:7 NLT

It was a day like every other. The lame man arrived with the help of his family to spend his waking hours begging at the temple gate. Crippled from birth, it was about the only thing he could do to survive. It was the last formal prayer time of the day when the Jews would make their sacrifices and often give alms to the poor. As Peter and John arrived at the gate, the lame man asked for money, hoping for a coin or two. Imagine his utter amazement when Peter said, "I don't have any silver or gold for you. But I'll give you what I have. In the name of Jesus Christ the Nazarene, get up and walk!" (See Acts 3:6)

Are you sitting at that gate this morning, hoping you will receive a bit of joy or encouragement from someone passing by? Remember this. No human being can meet your needs— only God can. Are you placing your hope horizontally rather than vertically? The lame man "looked up" and received much more than he ever dreamed. This day, put your hope in God.

God, today I choose to put my hope in you, as you are the source of everything I need. Forgive me for looking elsewhere and help me to keep my eyes on you.

The ideal temperature for sleep is 60–67 degrees fahrenheit depending on personal preference.
Our body temperatures decrease as we fall asleep, so we can help ourselves fall asleep faster by setting the thermostat within this optimal range.

PUT ON YOUR BELT

*Stand firm then, with the belt of truth buckled
around your waist, with the breastplate of
righteousness in place.*

EPHESIANS 6:14 NIV

Every single day, courts are in session all over the world. The
ultimate goal of the process is to discern the truth, which may
set the defendant free or send him to jail. There is power in
truth but also power in the enemy's deception. Wearing the
belt of truth enables us to discern between the two. For the
Roman soldier, the belt was the home for his sword. It held
up his heavy breastplate, and it provided a place to tuck in his
tunic to prevent him from tripping. The truth of God's Word
does that for us spiritually. It can be wielded like a sword
against the deception of the enemy, and it can keep us from
falling into sin. The Word holds us together.

Have you put on your belt of truth today? Spend some time
in God's Word and soak in the truth found there. Don't rely
on any other source to guide you. Stand firm in the truth!

God, I am so grateful that you have provided the standard of absolute and unfailing truth for my life. I put on the belt this morning and look forward to a joy-filled and victorious day.

Can't remember where you left your keys? Eat breakfast! The most important meal of the day is shown to improve cognitive function, particularly activities that are related to memory and performance.

SLIPPING

I cried out, "I am slipping!"
but your unfailing love, O LORD, supported me.
When doubts filled my mind,
your comfort gave me renewed hope and cheer.

PSALM 94:18-19 NLT

If you live in a climate where ice and snow abound, you probably have slipped and fallen at least once. As you know, it happens quickly! You are bustling along when suddenly out go your feet and down you go. After assessing for injury, you quickly look around to see if anyone noticed. It is humiliating to be so out of control.

Life can sometimes blindside us with difficulties that completely throw us off balance. And, yes, it can be humbling to realize that we do not have control over much in our lives. Without God's support, we will take a tumble. Satan's plan for us is to slip and fall into anger, fear, depression, and disbelief. Cry out to God this morning; hang on to him tightly, and he will keep you from falling.

This morning, God, I cry out to you for support. I am unsure if I can keep my feet under me as I deal with this unexpected circumstance. Thank you for your comfort that renews my hope.

Maine produces more blueberries than anywhere else in the world. Blueberries are rich in antioxidants, which help protect against memory loss, boost focus, fight cancer, aid weight loss, combat aging, and more. Add a handful of this superfood to your oatmeal or smoothie for an antioxidant boost.

THE GOD OF ALL COMFORT

*Praise be to the God and Father of our
Lord Jesus Christ, the Father of compassion
and the God of all comfort.*

2 CORINTHIANS 1:3 NIV

Comfort is what our hearts cry out for in times of trouble or sorrow. We need someone to sit beside us, to listen to our story, to put a comforting arm around our shoulders, and to just be there. Our friends and families, though they love us, are limited by time and resources. They cannot always meet our needs. This is the moment to look to God—the source of compassion and comfort. Read the Psalms and hang on to the promises found there. God does not grow tired or weary of us; he is always near.

Have a great day today—yes, even joyful! You have a God who loves you. He is full of compassion, and he is the source of all comfort. Run to him this morning and let him soothe your troubled soul.

Father, you are my God—full of compassion
and eager to comfort my soul. I give you my distress
and ask that you would bind up my heart. I begin this
day with your strength.

A typical breakfast in eastern China can include items
such as dumplings, rice and vegetable soup, fried sponge
cake, porridge, and steamed creamy custard buns, also
known as Lai Wong Bao. The main ingredients in the
custard of these buns are milk and egg yolk,
which gives the custard a sweet flavor.

WAIT FOR THE LORD

I wait for the LORD, my soul waits,
and in his word I hope;
my soul waits for the Lord
more than watchmen for the morning,
more than watchmen for the morning.

PSALM 130:5-6 ESV

We live in a fast culture: instant messaging, fast food, high speed internet, automated everything! The quicker, the shorter, the better we like it. Waiting is just not on our list of favorite things to do. We are used to getting things done in a relatively efficient fashion, yet when we pray, God seems to be on an entirely different timetable. He often asks us to wait. Why? Because God is more interested in developing our character than he is in instant messaging. Patience, endurance, faithfulness, and perseverance are developed in the waiting.

Are you frustrated by unanswered prayers this morning? God is setting the stage, working in other people's lives, and arranging circumstances until just the right time. Your answer will come. Don't be passive in the waiting; pray, read the Word, and hang on to the promises of God. You can do it!

God, please help me to be patient as I wait for you to move in my life. Nothing is wasted. You work everything for my good. I trust you to do what is best.

Whether you call it a roundabout, a traffic circle, a rotary, or something else, lots of drivers believe these intersections add time to our commutes. However, traffic patterns show that, on average, roundabouts actually save time.

BREATHE AGAIN

Give all your worries to him, because he cares for you.

1 PETER 5:7 NCV

Anxiety can take your breath away. It comes in all sorts of forms: an unpaid bill, a sick friend, or an uncertain future. When we feel overcome with anxiety, it can paralyze us. Our entire world stops, and we slowly sink lower and lower into worry and fear. Sometimes when we feel anxious, we try to push back those feelings by eating our favorite foods or treating ourselves to a day of shopping. Maybe we even turn to friends. But we often try to deal with anxiety alone because it can be so scary. Who could possibly understand?

God *does* understand, and he is not judging us in our struggles. If we lay our worries before him, he is quick to comfort us. If anxiety is pressing into you this morning, turn to the Lord. Wash yourself in his holy Word. Allow his promises to comfort you and bring you peace.

God, when anxiety comes and threatens to paralyze me, whisper your words of comfort and promises of peace. Thank you that when I trust you, when I lean into you, I can breathe again.

Stitching Gouda Oogst, a woman from the Netherlands, earned the title for the "World's Largest Waffle" in 2013. Her waffle measured eight feet long and weighed 110 pounds.

MY HEALER

O Lord my God, I cried to you for help,
and you have healed me.

Psalm 30:2 ESV

We all find comfort in various things. Maybe it's a good book in front of a warm fire, or it could be that pasta dish your mother makes. For some, it's the familiar smell of pine and early morning mist. When we are sick, sad, scared, or worried, we all long to be surrounded by the people or things that comfort us. We want our needs to be seen and taken care of in a loving and gentle way. When we face affliction, we are desperate for a healer to come quickly.

We can always take comfort in God. He loves to come and take care of us in our weakest moments. Let him be the warm blanket wrapped around you this morning. Let him be the sun shining on your face. He is the one who longs to hold you close, chase away your fears, and heal your fevers. All you have to do is ask, and he will be there.

Jesus, thank you that you are always close,
and that you make your comforting presence
known to me. Thank you that
you are my healer.

A popular Venezuelan breakfast choice is an arepa.

Arepas are flat corn cakes that come with a

variety of fillings, such as cheese, ham, beef, chicken,

and fish. This tasty dish is also served as a snack

or a side dish.

DON'T BE AFRAID

"Peace I leave with you; my peace I give you. I do not give to you as the world gives. Do not let your hearts be troubled and do not be afraid."

JOHN 14:27 NIV

Watch the news for a few seconds, and you'll see just how scary the world is. There is war, pain, chaos, and hatred. Add all that to our own reasons for worrying—money problems, relationships, uncertain futures—and it's enough to rob us of our sleep and wake feeling completely unrested.

God wants to calm your spirit. He does not want you to live in fear, but in full faith that he is the ruler of the world. Regardless of the outside noise and disharmony this morning, in God's hands is the gift of peace. Let go, relax, and breathe. He is in control of every situation—even if you can't see or understand.

Thank you, Jesus, for your gift of peace.
When the world is in chaos, and there are so many
reasons to fear, you gently whisper not to be afraid.
I am so thankful that you settle and calm my spirit.

Not only are we sleeping less, but we're also struggling
to stay asleep. Thirty-five percent of us report that
we wake up in the middle of the night at least three
times a week, and of those who wake, forty-three
percent report having difficulty falling back asleep.

TEMPORARY STRUGGLES

"God blesses you who are hungry now,
for you will be satisfied.
God blesses you who weep now,
for in due time you will laugh."

LUKE 6:21 NLT

Sometimes it seems as if life will never get easier. We wake up with the same struggles and trials day after day. We grow weary of fighting the same battles. We wonder when we will find rest and relief. In our suffering, it can be difficult to see God's goodness, and we feel as if we will never experience joy or happiness again.

God promises that your trials and struggles are only temporary. He assures you that he will replace your aches and pains with happiness and laughter. It's in that promise that you can find comfort this morning.

Jesus, I am thankful that my struggles are only temporary. I am thankful that you promise to lift my pain and fill my heart with joy and peace. Thank you for comforting me this morning. I need your presence.

Most Europeans did not sleep through the night until the Industrial Age. In fact, both adults and children divided their sleep into two spans and would enjoy a quiet hour of wakefulness in between.

THE GATEWAY TO LIFE

*"Very truly I tell you, unless a kernel of wheat falls
to the ground and dies, it remains only a single seed.
But if it dies, it produces many seeds."*

JOHN 12:24 NIV

Fall in the northern United States is spectacular. The intense
colors and the crisp, cool air is a reminder that winter is on
its way. The dying leaves waft beautifully to the ground in
gentle submission to their maker's plan. It's a time of death.
Jesus spoke of this principle in John 12 when he said there
must be death in order for life to come forth. Paul testified
in Galatians 2 that he had been crucified with Christ and
was now dead to self, sin, and the world. He no longer
lived—Christ lived in and through him. The power of sin
was gone, and new life was born.

Are you hanging onto something this morning that Christ
is asking you to bring to the cross? Sin and willfulness must
die for resurrection to occur. Death is the gateway to life, so
let go of whatever it is you shouldn't be holding onto and
embrace new life!

Thank you, Jesus, for loving me enough to die for me and then to invite me to share in that death. In that place, new life begins. I choose to lay down my own agenda at the foot of the cross this morning. Thank you for raising me to newness of life!

Our brains are busy when we sleep. In addition to countless other jobs, our brains use the time that we're asleep to strengthen, reorganize, and restructure our memories—all of which are important in order to function optimally the next day.

CREATED FOR A PURPOSE

We know that in all things God works for
the good of those who love him, who have
been called according to his purpose.

ROMANS 8:28 NIV

A life without purpose feels hopeless—mundane at best.
Without a specific goal or direction, it is easy to question
ourselves. Why do I get up in the morning? Why am I
working so hard? Does my life have significance or meaning?
Am I making an impact on the world? The questions will be
endless because we were created for a purpose. We weren't
created to float mindlessly throughout our days. When we
live that way, we feel a deep sense of emptiness and loneliness.

We were created first to love God. It's in our love for him
that we will find our reason for living. In loving him, our
lives are transformed. The more we fix our eyes on him, the
more we desire to reflect him. The more we reflect him, the
less empty we feel. Worldly possessions lose their luster,
selfishness diminishes, and we find fulfillment, contentment,
and *purpose* in living for him.

Jesus, when I feel lost, let me find fulfillment in simply loving and serving you. May my contentment in life come from knowing you. Draw me close to you this morning and show me that you have an incredible purpose for my life.

The most important ingredients in a healthy breakfast are fiber and protein. Not only are they low in fat, but they also keep you feeling fuller for longer. Foods like oatmeal and whole grain breads contain both of these important macronutrients.

COMPASSION THAT NEVER CEASES

The steadfast love of the LORD never ceases,
his mercies never come to an end;
they are new every morning;
great is your faithfulness.

LAMENTATIONS 3:22-23 NRSV

Has anyone shown you compassion when you needed it? The answer is "yes" for all of mankind. God is a compassionate God, and his compassions will never fail. Others may have failed you many times, but God will not fail you. Not only will his compassion not fail, but it is also regenerated *every single morning*. Fresh compassion pours over your life and your circumstances each day.

God's steadfast love this morning says, "I understand what you are going through. I know this is hard." He doesn't point from a distance and ridicule you for not being tough enough. No, he comes alongside you in your suffering, and he promises that he will neither leave nor forsake you in your hour of need.

Father, thank you that when I am at my weakest,
you are there. You have compassion toward me.
Thank you for your steady, kind love this morning.
Help me to walk in your new mercies.

Social media isn't just for socializing anymore.
Now, 85 percent of people read Twitter and Facebook
as resources for their morning news, and 28 percent
of iPhone users read their Twitter feed even
before getting out of bed.

SATISFIED

Because your love is better than life,
my lips will glorify you.
I will praise you as long as I live,
and in your name I will lift up my hands.
I will be fully satisfied as with the richest of foods;
with singing lips my mouth will praise you.

PSALM 63:3-5 NIV

There are times in our lives when we really need answers or a breakthrough, and sometimes we just want to be blessed. Our loving Father says to simply ask. He wants to give us good gifts.

You might not want to ask for things because you feel they are too much or too specific. But God is able to handle your requests — he won't give you things that can be used for selfish gain or things that bring you harm. He knows what is best for you. His love is better than life itself, and he knows exactly how to satisfy you this morning.

God, there are many things that I need and many things that I want. I ask you for the things that are best for me. I know that you are a loving Father who answers me with kindness and with perfect wisdom.

According to market research, Honey Nut Cheerios is the best-selling cereal in the United States. Frosted Flakes places second, and Honey Bunches of Oats comes in third.

PROVISION FOR THE GENEROUS

May He who supplies seed to the sower, and bread for food, supply and multiply the seed you have sown and increase the fruits of your righteousness.

2 CORINTHIANS 9:10 NKJV

The beginning of generosity is provision. Just as a farmer requires seed for a harvest, we must also be provided with something to sow. God has supplied you with everything you need to help grow his kingdom. He will increase your resources as you diligently plant the seeds of faith.

As God multiplies your resources, he will also increase the harvest; that is, the good that comes from what you have sown. He gives to you generously that you might be generous. Be encouraged this morning to give from what he has given you and watch the blessings in your life increase.

Heavenly Father, you continue to supply me with all that I need. Help me to sow my seeds of faith, so that I might see growth in my life and in the lives of others. Lead me to generosity, so that your work will be done on earth as it is in heaven.

Over 7,500 varieties of apples are produced around the world, and Red Delicious apples are the most popularly grown. Apples are the second favorite fruit in the United States (after bananas) and are composed of 18 percent air. Because of their high water content, apples help your mouth produce more saliva, and the saliva helps wash away bacteria that can cause tooth discoloration.

CONTINUAL PRAISE

From the rising of the sun to its going down
The Lord's name is to be praised.

PSALM 113:3 NKJV

What would it look like to be someone who praises God from the time you awaken each morning until the time you fall asleep each night? Not only would you be pleasing God as you worship him constantly, but you would also effect an incredible change in your personal outlook.

Intentional, continual praise can only result in intentional, continual joy. When you choose to look at each moment as a moment in which to be thankful and worshipful, then you will find beauty, joy, and satisfaction in each moment.

God, I praise you for your love for me.
I pray that you would help me to be someone who
praises you all day, every day. I pray that you would
cultivate in me an appreciation of your goodness
and a longing to worship you constantly.

Early birds are more likely to be deemed "problem
solvers" since they are also more likely to use
their morning time to organize their thoughts and
prepare for their days. Those who rise later tend
to jump from one thought to another.

BLOOM WHERE YOU ARE PLANTED

"They are those who, hearing the word,
hold it fast in an honest and good heart,
and bear fruit with patience."

LUKE 8:15 ESV

Most of us want to make a significant mark at some point in our lifetimes. It's comforting to believe that the routine of our ordinary lives is merely preparation for the really big assignment that is surely just around the corner—you know, the lofty thing, the high calling, the noble assignment that undoubtedly lies directly ahead.

Then one day in a moment of quiet, God whispers, "This is it. What you are doing is what I've called you to do. Do your work, love your neighbor, serve people, seek me first, and everything you long for in your heart will be fulfilled. Be faithful right where I've put you. You don't need to accomplish great things for me. Just be." Can you hear that whisper this morning?

God, I long for significance. I want my life to matter. Help me to understand that it's not what I do for you that is important. What's important is who I am and whose I am. Help me to be faithful in the assignment you have given me right now.

Morning glory flowers earn their name from their early morning blooming. They also possess medicinal properties. Native Americans scraped and ate the root of this plant to relieve stomach discomfort.

STARTING OVER

Praise the LORD!
Oh, give thanks to the LORD, for He is good!
For His mercy endures forever.

PSALM 106:1 NKJV

Have you ever wished you could start over? It would be so great to turn back the clock, reverse a decision, and do something differently. There is so much wisdom in looking back! There are some things we can redo, like tweak a recipe or rip a seam, but most often, the important, big decisions can't be changed.

When it comes to spiritual matters, God tells us that we can start over every morning because his mercies will be there. Whatever went awry the day before, whatever mess we made from poor choices, we can begin the next day with a completely clean slate! Our part in the transaction may require repentance of sin or forgiving someone—perhaps even ourselves. Bathed in his mercies, we can begin each day squeaky clean!

God, I am so grateful that your love and your mercies never end. You extend them to me brand new every morning. Great is your faithfulness!

The weekends are often considered a time to catch up on some sleep, but scientists have learned that sleeping in on the weekends actually throws our bodies off their internal clocks, making waking up on Monday morning more difficult.

ABIDING LOVE

Satisfy us in the morning with your unfailing love,
that we may sing for joy and be glad all our days.

Psalm 90:14 NIV

Think of brand-new love where the excitement and
enthusiasm are almost overwhelming. Where you wouldn't
miss an opportunity to steal another moment together.
Whether a budding romance, a precious new pet, or even a
fresh health and fitness plan, that initial feeling may or may
not take root.

Make sure this morning that you are rooted firmly in your
relationship with Jesus. Let the joy of discovering him give
way to the deeper joy of knowing him and walking with him
each day. There is nothing that compares to the satisfying
love of God.

God, my heart overflows with thankfulness as I consider all you've done for me. Strengthen my faith as I live my life in your deep, abiding strength and love. I sink my roots down right here and into my love for you.

Breakfast in the 1600s was usually leftover cheese and bread or stewed grains. It wasn't until the mid to late 1800s that people started eating what we would now call breakfast foods.

ACCEPTANCE

"I have brought you glory on earth by finishing the work you gave me to do."

JOHN 17:4 NIV

As we walk in love, we will see fruit develop from what we do. We bring life and joy, truth and gentleness. We bring our gifts and ambitions. Sometimes this is met with delight and gratitude. Other times people don't understand our intentions. We may sow our gifts faithfully and never see good come of it. You may be feeding the poor and feeling heartbroken that there is not enough water. You may be clothing the naked and weeping that their bills won't be paid this month.

The point is this: You are being faithful. God is proud of you. And though the world around you may not understand what you are doing, and though you may not understand the world around you, Jesus has everything under control. He is making beautiful things in and with you. That is enough. Just walk with him in faith this morning.

God, there is so much of the world that I don't
understand. Some of it I don't want to know.
Make me bold to trust you and to know that everything
will be okay as I rest in you and walk in life.

After water, the most consumed beverage in the world
is tea. You may be surprised that the answer isn't
coffee, but tea was around for almost 3000 years
before coffee. Its popularity could be explained by the
simplicity of production—it only requires mixing dried
leaves in warm water.

ORIGIN OF STRENGTH

"People do not live by bread alone, but by every word that comes from the mouth of God."

Matthew 4:4 NLT

When Jesus was tempted, he had been fasting in the wilderness for forty days and forty nights. He wasn't consuming any calories during that time. Instead, he devoted all his energy to communing with the Father and to gaining strength through their relationship. At the end of his fast, Satan tried to tempt him. Jesus withstood authentic temptation and never gave in.

It's interesting how God prepared Jesus for this trial. He didn't have Jesus attend a conference, read a self-help book, or participate in a healing service. Instead, he led his Son to be physically weaker so that Jesus could fully rely on the Father. Jesus had been on a 40-day diet of love, affirmation, and encouragement. He wasn't weakened by his lack of food. In fact, he made it clear that food alone wasn't what made him strong. While your breakfast might be wonderful this morning, it isn't food that sustains you—it's God's power in you that will keep you going.

Father, thank you that I don't live on bread alone. Help me eat what I need to be strong in you. Help me to live by every Word that comes from your mouth.

A healthy breakfast will help keep your body energized throughout the day. You can maximize your vitamin and mineral intake by eating whole grains, lean protein, fruits, and vegetables in the morning. Try to cut added sugars and opt for foods such as oatmeal, eggs, and fruit smoothies instead.